Standin' Tall® with HONESTY

by Janeen Brady

Series Includes

1. Obedience
★ 2. Honesty
3. Forgiveness
4. Work
5. Courage
6. Happiness
7. Gratitude
8. Love
9. Service
10. Cleanliness
11. Self-Esteem
12. Dependability

©Copyright 1981 by Janeen Brady. All rights reserved. No part of this book may be reproduced in any form. Printed in the United States of America.

Hello there. Look what I have.

✶ **What is it?**

What does it look like?

✶ **Like a treasure box. What's in it?**

 What do you think is in my treasure box?
Rubies, emeralds, nuggets of gold.
What will we find when I undo the locks?
Silver, diamonds, all it can hold.
What's the best treasure you can imagine
　of all the treasures on earth?
Tell me, how much is my fabulous treasure box worth?

Oh, I'm so excited. Stand back a little. There's magic in this box. I can feel it.

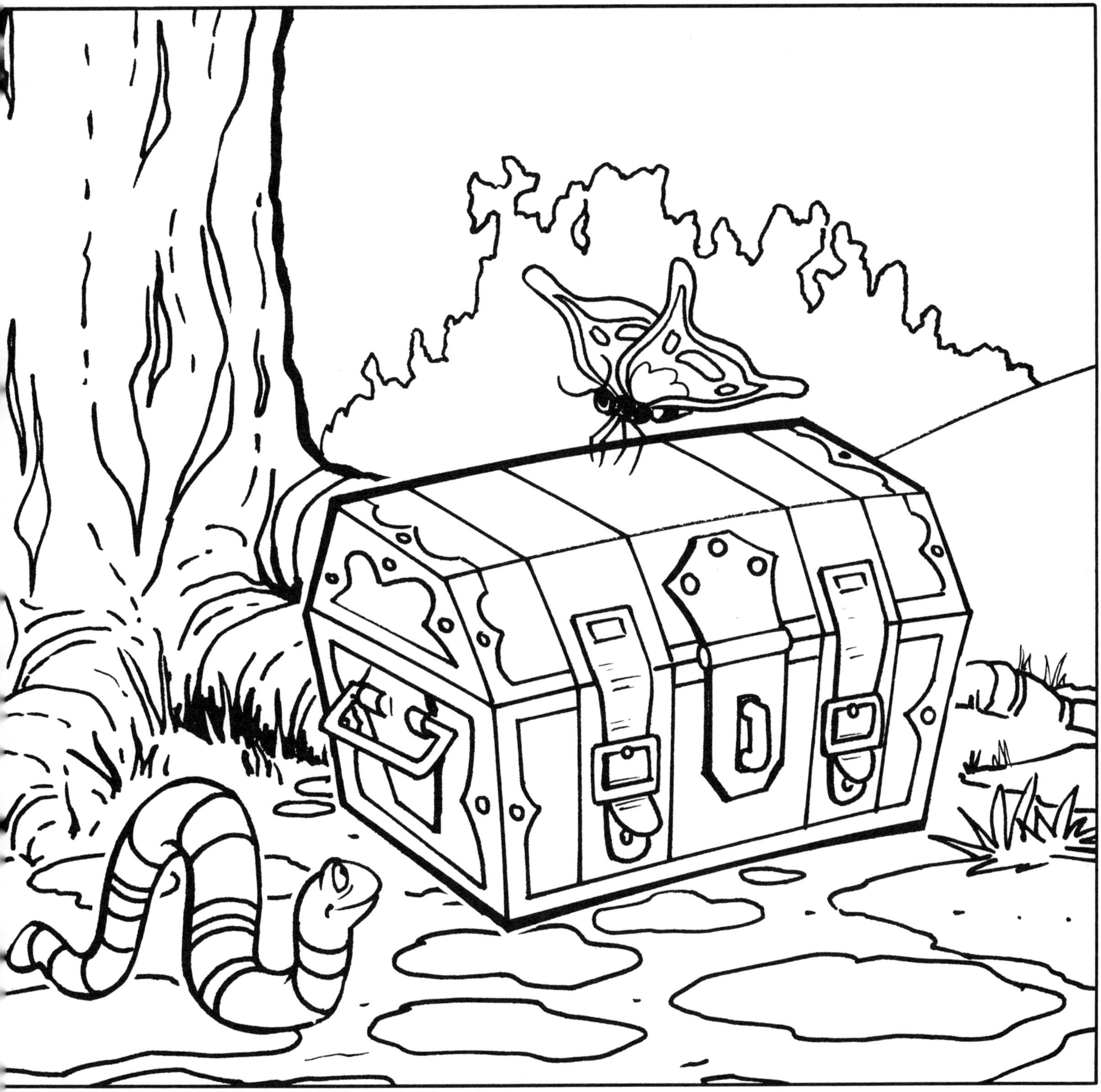

★ It's empty, there isn't any treasure.

Oh, but wait! there's something in the corner.

★ It's just an old piece of paper.

Let's see what it says: Whosoever hath honor hath the greatest treasure of all.

★ What?

Do you know what it means to have honor?

★ Well, I guess it means telling the truth.

That's the idea. A person with honor is one who has learned the difference between right and wrong and chooses to do what's right.

★ The paper says a person who has honor has the greatest treasure. Does that mean having honor is better than having gold and rubies?

Yes.

★ Ah, anybody can tell the truth. I'd rather have a treasure box full of diamonds any day.

You could do an experiment and find out if you really would rather have diamonds than honor. Try telling the truth all day long today and see what happens.

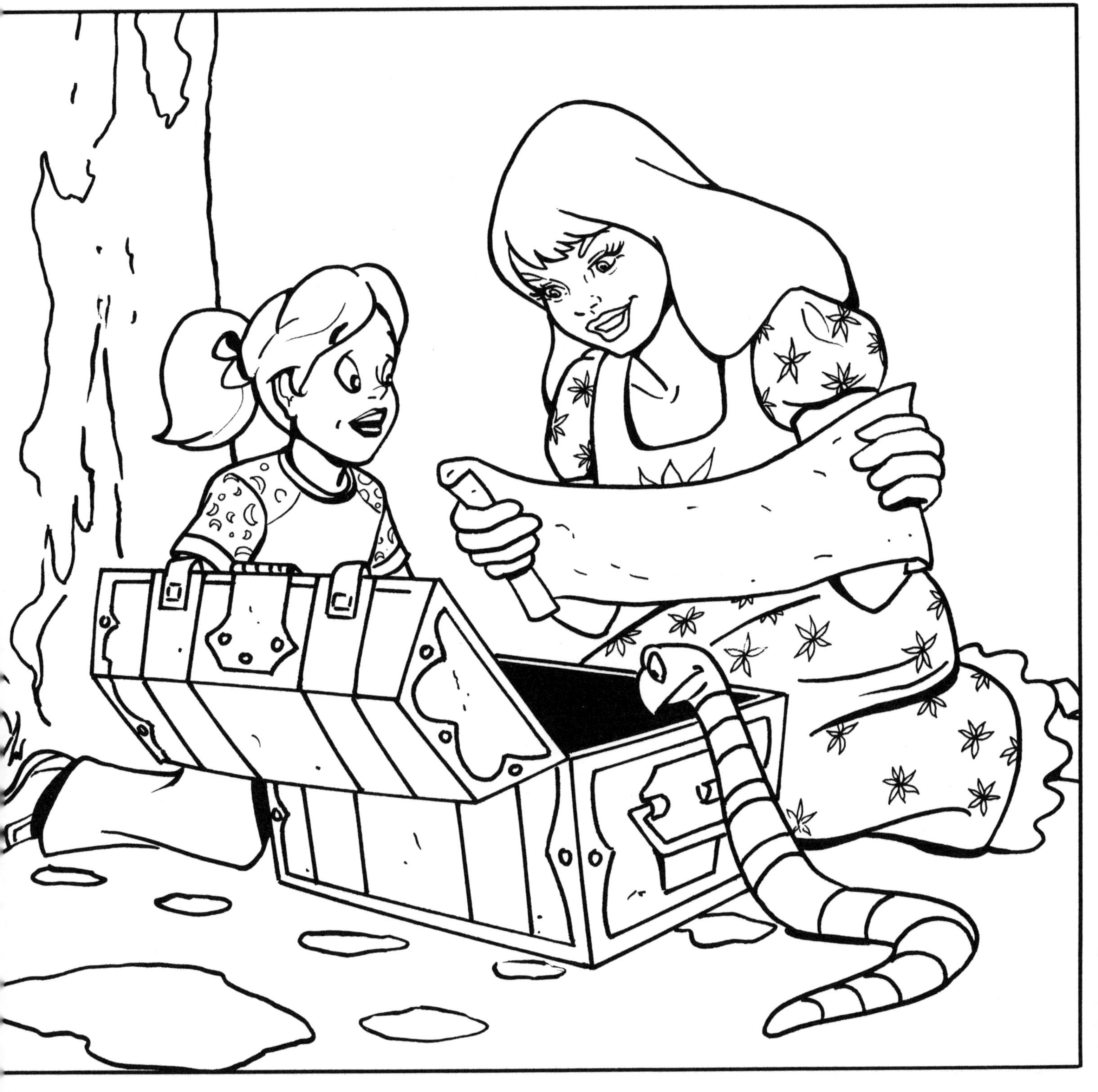

★ **Well, okay, but I've got to go now. My friends are here and we're going to play ball. 'Bye.**

 Throw the ball, then catch the ball, then throw it high in the air.
Throw the ball, then catch the ball, then throw the ball but take care.
Kick the ball, and then run and get it, then
Kick the ball, put some muscle in it, then
Throw the ball, then catch the ball, then throw it high in the air.
Throw the ball, then catch the ball, then throw the ball but take. . .

SECOND CHILD: You knocked the ball right through Mr. Robinson's window, and he's the meanest man on the block.

THIRD CHILD: We've got to get out of here.

★ **Wait for me!**

"Whosoever hath honor hath the greatest treasure of all."

★ **That's what was in the treasure box. Oh . . . oh . . . never mind. You go without me. I've got to stay and tell Mr. Robinson I broke his window.**

SECOND CHILD: Are you crazy?

THIRD CHILD: He's going to be really mad.

★ **I know, but I've got to find out if it's true about the treasure box.**

THIRD CHILD: What's she talking about?

SECOND CHILD: I don't know, but I'm getting out of here. Here comes Mr. Robinson.

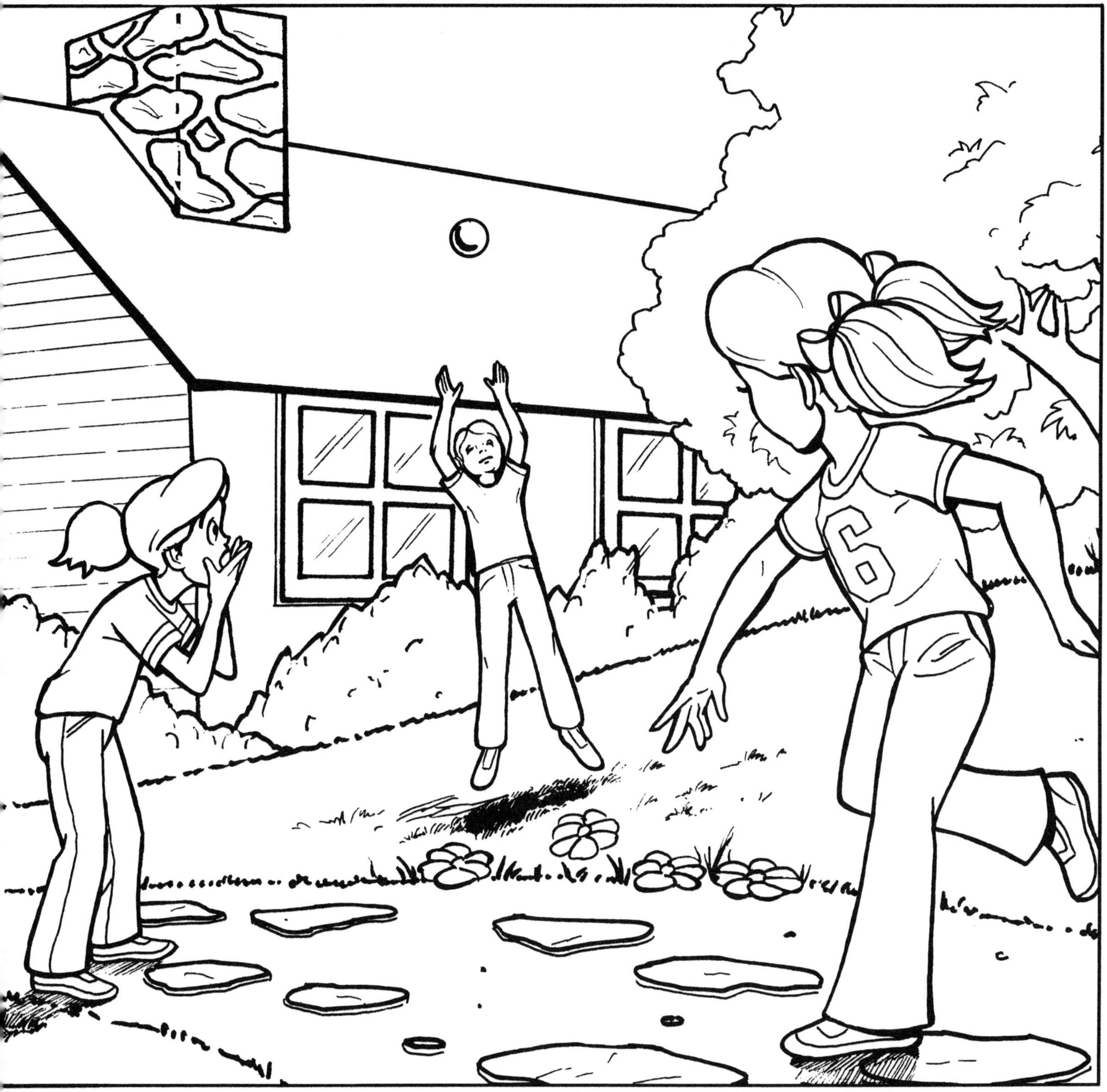

Who broke my window?
Telling the truth isn't going to be easy.
Glass, every place you look.
Who broke my window?
Why is my stomach all nervous and queasy?
Aha, some kid's ball.

Who can the little culprit be?
Who threw this ball, did someone see?
He's going to be so mad at me, I'm scared.

Who broke my window?
I know it's going to be hard to be honest.
I guess I'll never know
Who broke my window.
But I've just got to live up to my promise.
Kids these days, they don't care.

Mr. Robinson, Mr. Robinson!
What a horrible mess.
I broke your window with my ball, and I've come to confess.

You knew I'd be angry.
Yes.
Aren't you afraid?
Yes.
You'll have to pay for the mess you've made.
But I'm proud of you child for you have displayed
HONOR!
The stuff from which heroes are made.
I TOLD THE TRUTH!!

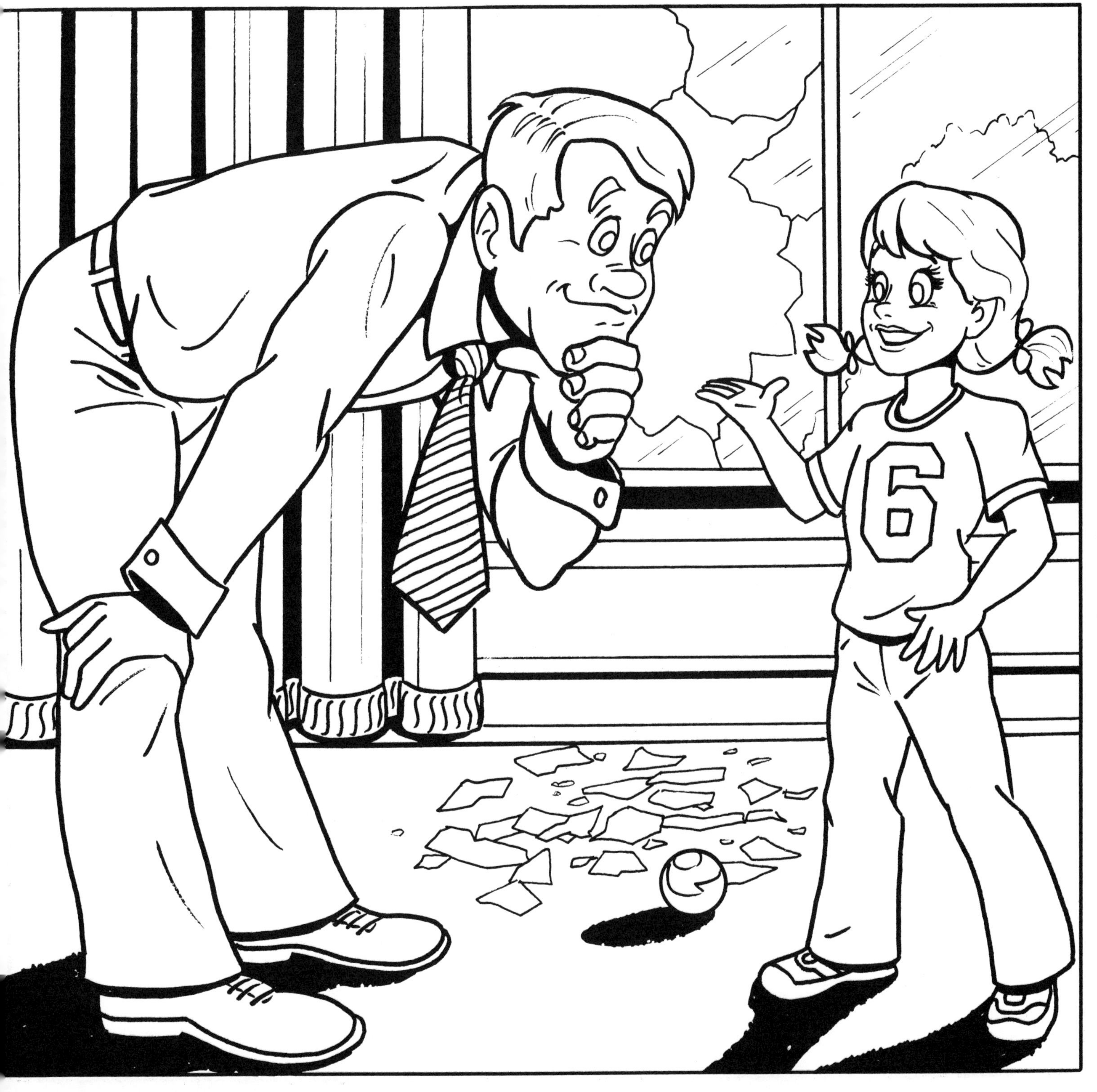

It's not always easy to tell the truth.

★ **But I feel so good inside.**

Would you trade that feeling for a dollar?

★ **I don't think so.**

How about for a diamond?

★ **Well...Oh, oh, I've got to go or I'll be late for school.**

 Hurry, hurry, walk a little faster, faster,
Hurry, hurry, maybe even run.
Hurry, hurry, walk a little faster, faster,
Hurry, hurry, school's about begun.
Climb the steps: one, two, three, four, five, six, seven, eight, nine.
Open the door. Pull with both hands and you'll get there on time.

Hurry, hurry, walk a little faster, faster,
Hurry now you're almost to your room.
Hurry, hurry, walk a little faster, faster,
Hurry, hurry, school is starting soon.
Hang your coat upon a hook, reach and get your favorite book.
Now sit down and take a breath, mustn't run yourself to death.
Hurry, hurry, hurry, off to school.

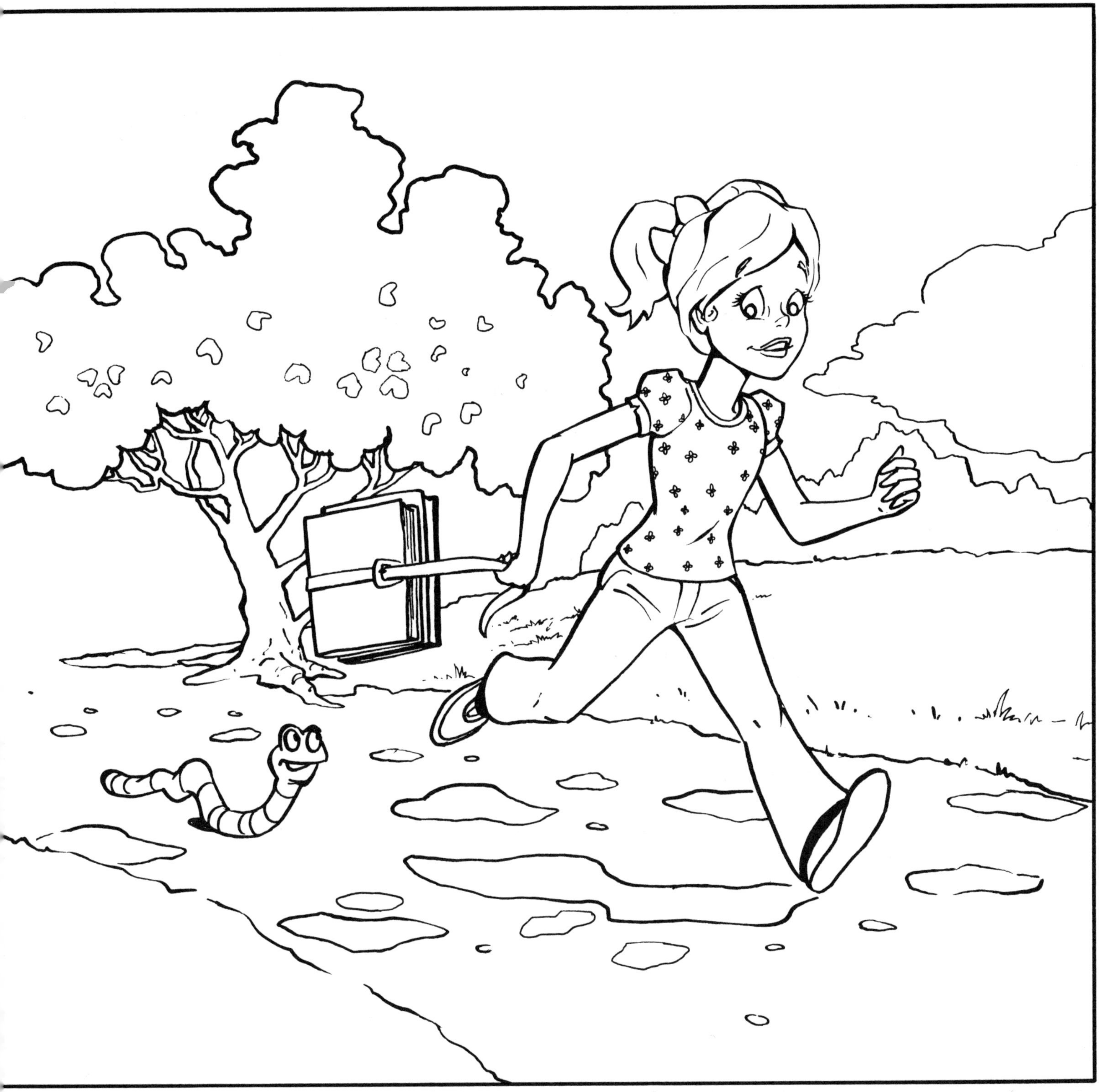

★ Oh, I made it.

TEACHER: Good morning children. I hope you all studied your spelling because it's time for our test.

★ I'll bet I get all the answers right. I worked hard on these words.

TEACHER: Get out your papers and pencils. Remember, no one look on anyone else's paper for the answers. Number one, truth—always tell the truth.

★ That's easy. Truth...T-R-U-T-H.

TEACHER: Number two, pure—a heart that is pure will never lie.

★ Pure...P-U-R-E.

TEACHER: Number three, honest—you can always believe a person who is honest.

★ Honest...H-O-N-E-S-T.

TEACHER: Number four, honor—a person with honor can be trusted.

★ Oh no, I dropped my pencil. I can't even reach it with my foot. I'll have to bend over and pick it up. I hope Miss Johnson doesn't see me.

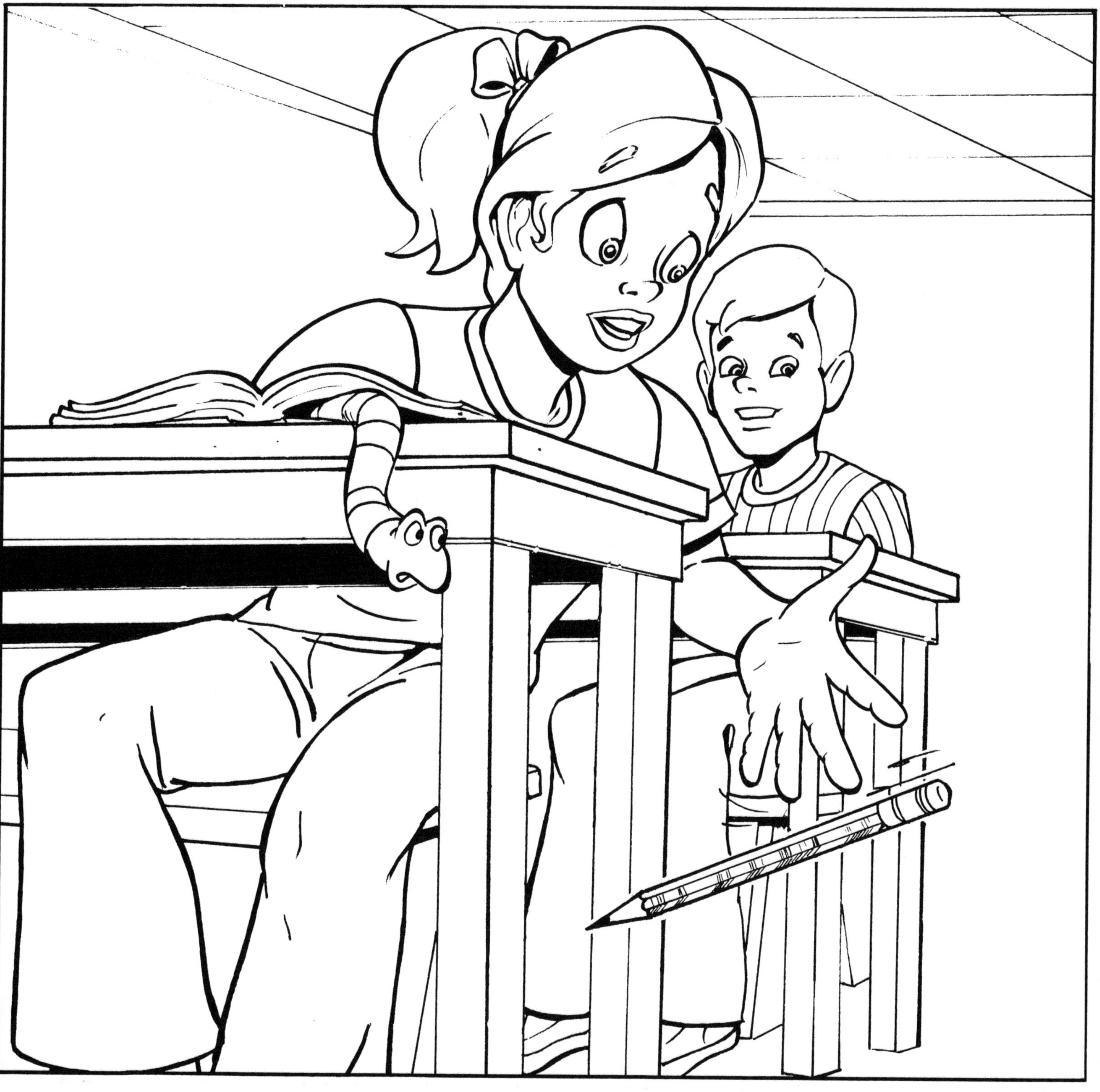

TEACHER: Why are you bending over? Are you looking on someone else's paper?

★ I dropped my pencil and I was picking it up.

TEACHER: You'd better give me your paper.

★ But I wasn't copying, honest.

TEACHER: Please give me your paper!

★ But I can spell all the words, and I always tell the truth.

SECOND CHILD: Yeah, today she told Mr. Robinson she broke his window.

THIRD CHILD: And he's really mean.

TEACHER: Is that true?

★ Yes.

TEACHER: This morning you told Mr. Robinson you broke his window?

★ Yes.

TEACHER: And now you're telling me the truth?

★ Uh huh.

TEACHER: Then you may have a second chance.

★ A second chance, because I told the truth? WOW!!!

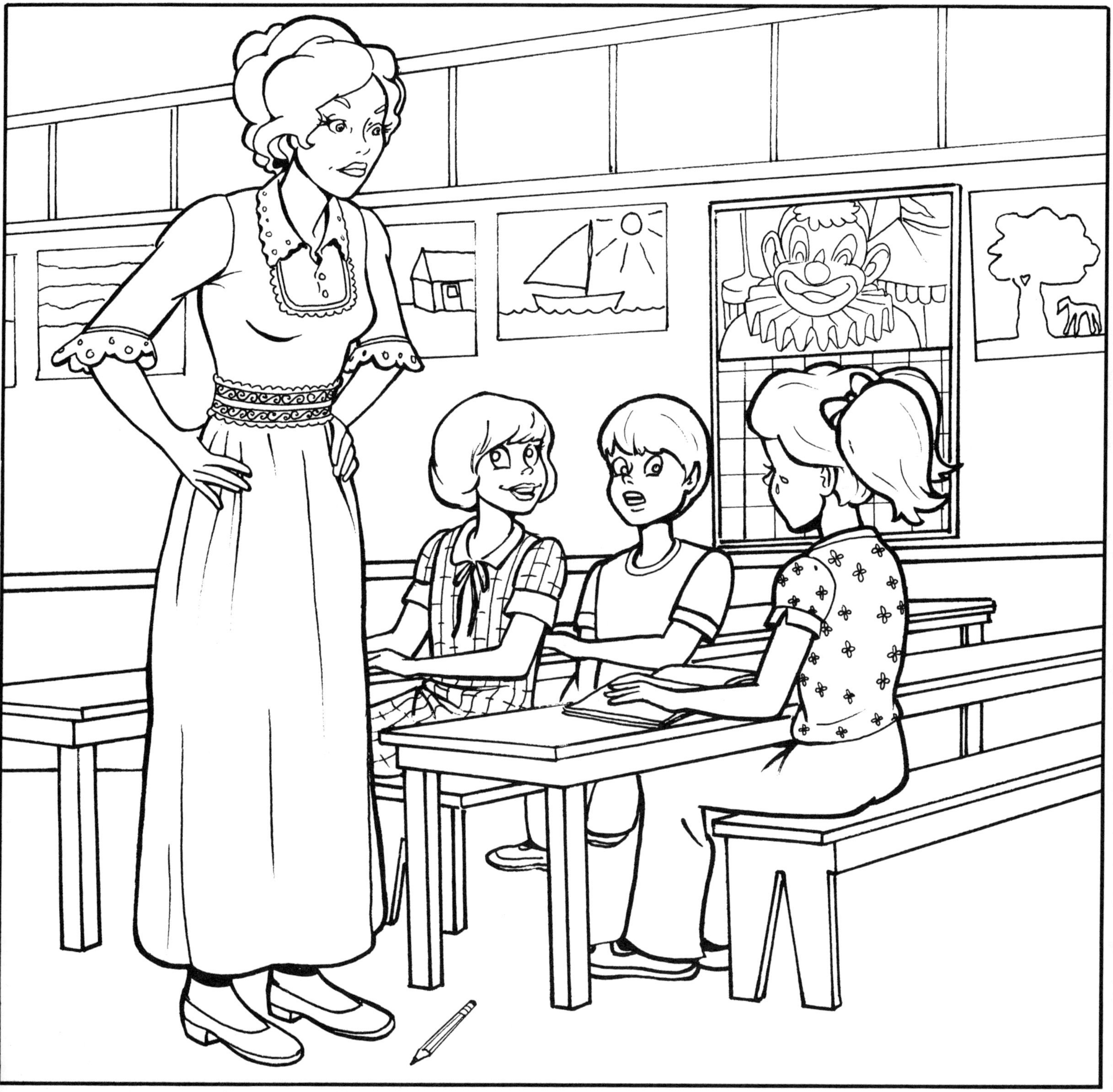

SECOND CHILD: Boy are you lucky!

★ **Yeah, telling the truth sure pays off!**

 I told the truth, I'm so happy I've got to start dancing.
I told the truth, feel so wonderful maybe I'll fly.
People I know are beginning to show they can trust me.
I'm learning now what's important and how my life must be.

I told the truth, and that's why I'm so joyfully singing.
I told the truth, and it feels like I'm starting to glow, so,
However hard it may be, I'll tell the truth honestly,
Wait and see there's going to be proof
That forevermore, I will evermore tell the truth.

Telling the truth is indeed like having a great treasure. Other people trust and believe you, and best of all you feel so good inside. You are true to yourself.

Now, let's see what happened to our friend on the way home from school.

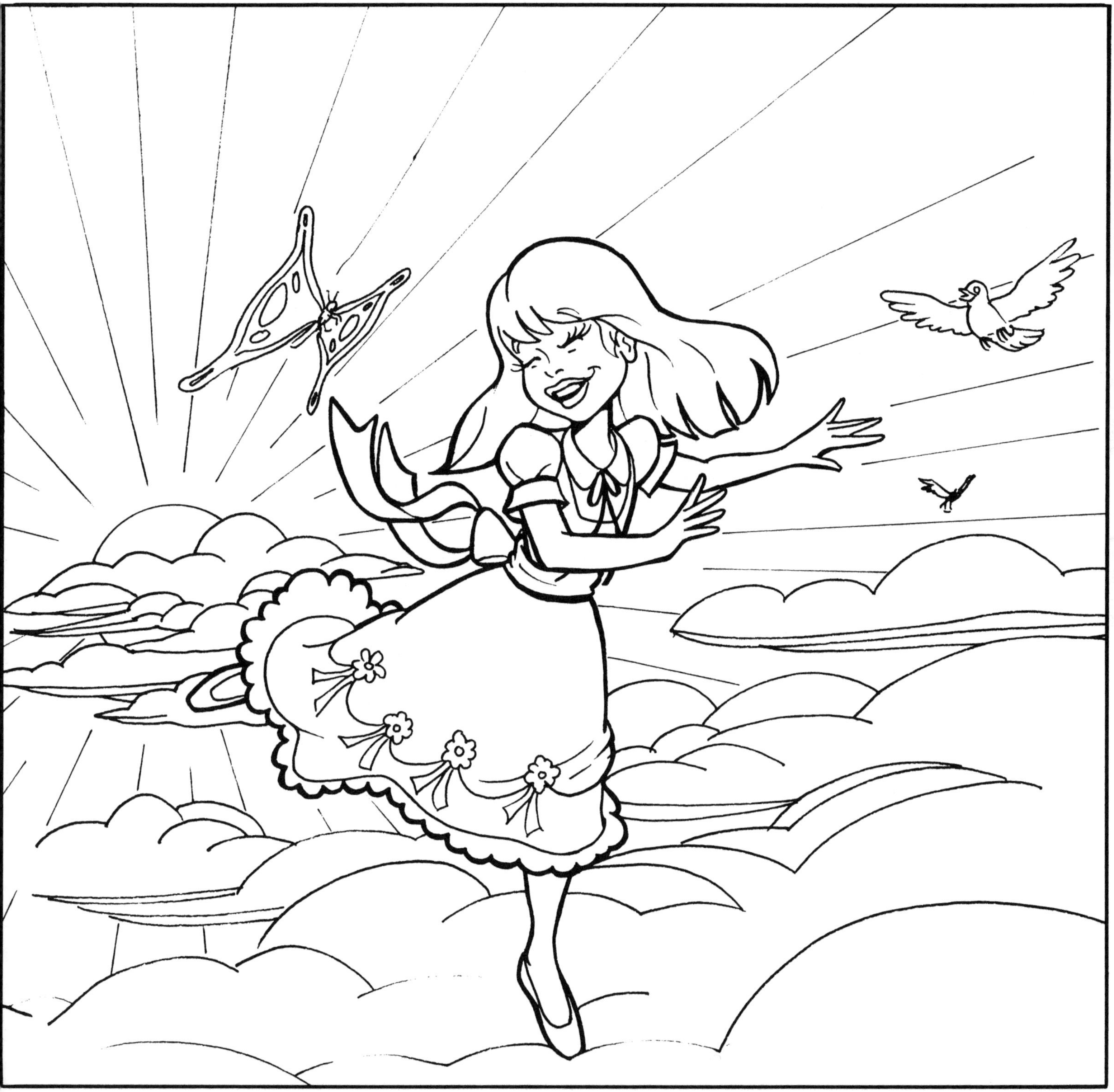

★ Those doughnuts in the bakery sure smell good. Let's see, yep, I still have my money from dad.

   CLERK: Hi, may I help you?

★ I want one of those big chocolate doughnuts please.

   CLERK: Sure thing. Here you go, and here's your change.

★ Thank you. MMM, I love doughnuts, and I still have some money left. I'd better count it. Five, six, seven, eight, nine...Hey, there's an extra quarter here! The clerk gave me back too much money. That will buy another doughnut. Wow, for lucky!!

   "Whosoever hath honor hath the greatest treasure of all."

★ It wasn't my fault she gave me too much change. If I don't tell her she'll never find out, and I can tell my mom I found the quarter, and I'll tell my...

   Wait, don't you see what's happening?

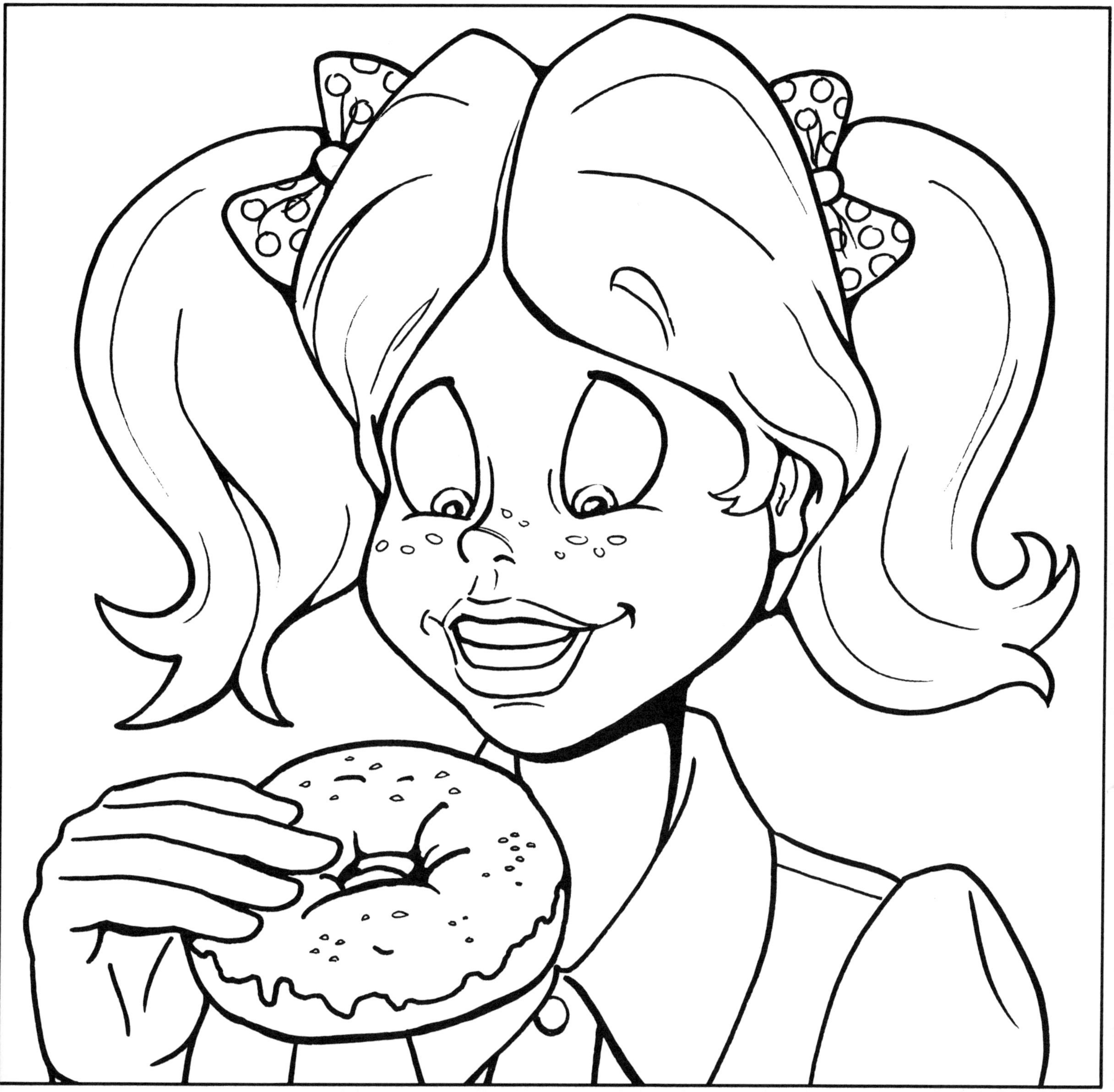

When you tell one lie it leads to another, so you tell two lies to cover
　　each other,
Then you tell three lies and, oh brother, you're in trouble up to your ears.
So you tell four lies to try to protect you, then you tell five lies
　　so folks won't suspect you,
Then you tell six lies and you collect a life filled with worries and fears.

'Cause you can't remember how many lies you've told when
　　half the things you say aren't true.
And sometime you'll trip up, you'll slip up and then whatever will
　　become of you?

Soon you'll lie and lie without even trying, and each lie you tell
　　will keep multiplying,
Till the whole wide world will know you're lying.
Then you'll be suspected, rejected, disliked, and you should.
When you lie, you're closing the door on everything good.
　　on everything good, on everything good.

★ **I don't want to be that kind of a person. I want to feel good about myself. I'm taking this quarter back right now.**

Children, can you pretend that you're our honest friend? When the music starts, skip back to the bakery, walk right up to the clerk and give the quarter back.

CLERK: Hi again. Do you want to buy another doughnut?

★ **Well...no...I think you gave me too much change.**

CLERK: Oh, you're right! That was an honest thing to do. You've really made my day. Thanks so much.

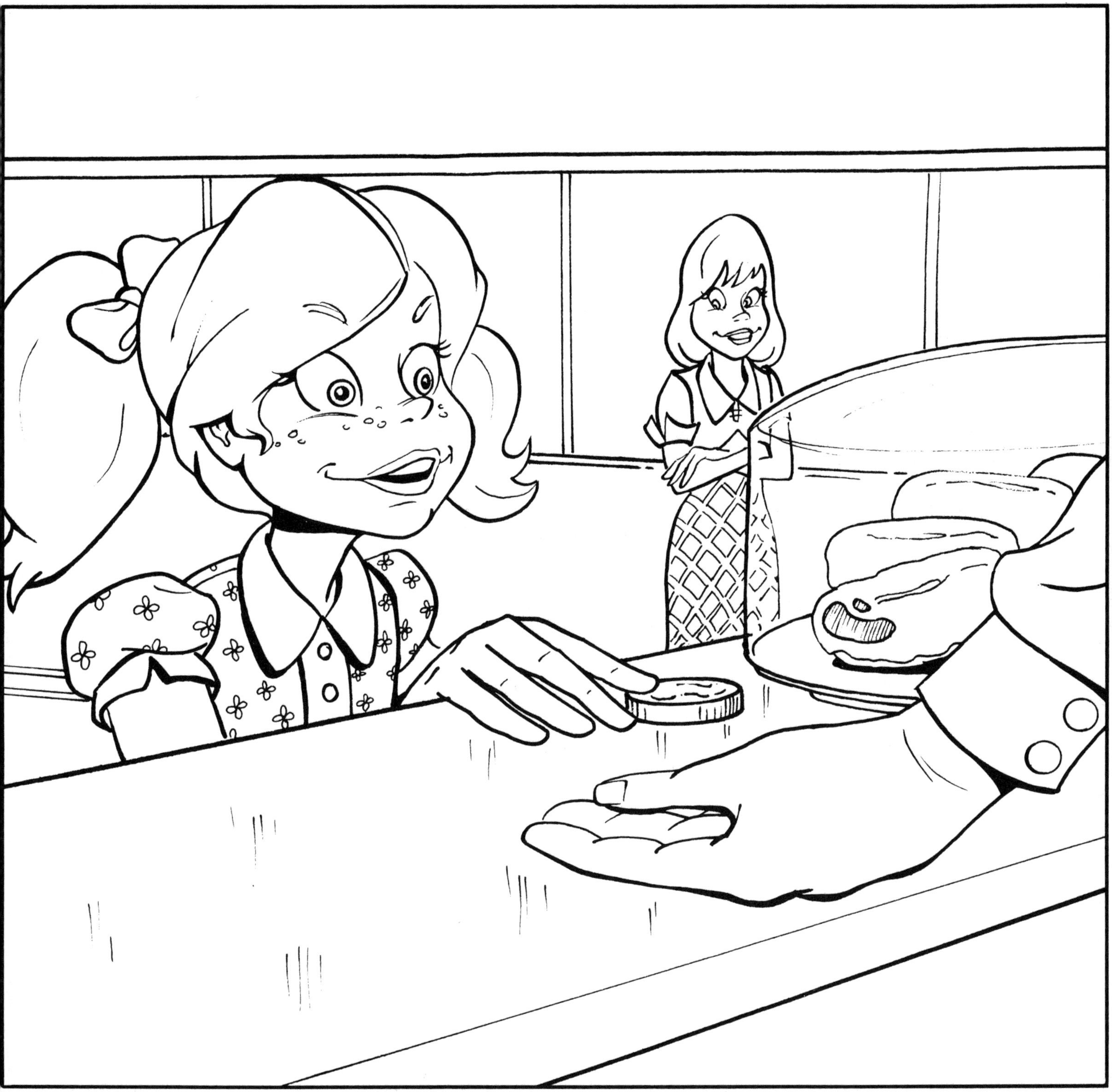

Now, how do you feel?

★ Just great!

I know, because you have discovered you'd rather have honor than doughnuts. Do you still feel the same about the diamonds and rubies?

★ Well, I'd still like to have a box full of treasure. But if I had to choose, I'd rather be an honest person. Besides, when I tell the truth I feel so good inside.

I told the truth, I'm so happy I've got to start dancing.
I told the truth, feel so wonderful maybe I'll fly.
People I know are beginning to show they can trust me.
I'm learning now what's important and how my life must be.

I told the truth, and that's why I'm so joyfully singing.
I told the truth and it feels like I'm starting to glow, so,
However hard it may be, I'll tell the truth honestly,
Wait and see, there's going to be proof
That forevermore I will evermore, evermore, evermore
Tell the truth!

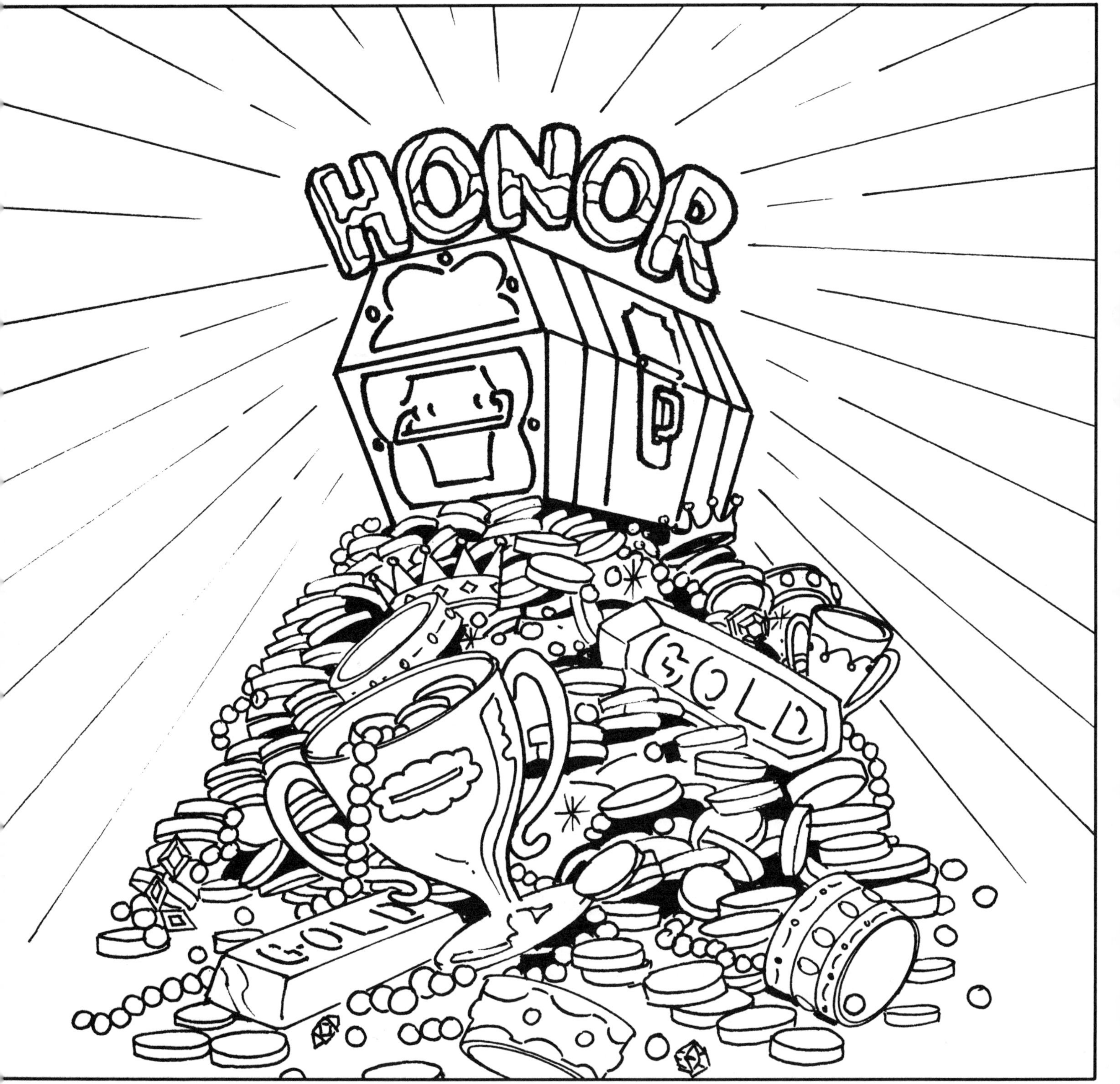
HONOR
GOLD
GOLD

Side A of each cassette contains the complete program. **Side B** repeats the same program but leaves out the lines of the main child in the story, giving the listener the chance to read along, saying aloud the missing lines and actually becoming a member of the cast. This fascinating activity helps older children with their reading and provides an excellent opportunity for development in dramatics.

Children can sing along with the songs, color the pictures and participate in still other activities as the story progresses.

A Product of BRITE MUSIC ENTERPRISES, INC.

Music and Dramatics recorded, engineered and mixed at Bonneville Media Communications.
Illustrations by Grant Wilson and Neil Galloway / Graphic production by Whipple & Associates.
Music arranged and conducted by Merrill Jenson.